An Order

Illustrated by Sarah Howell

Other Books by Sarah Howell on Amazon

On The Day You Were Baptized
On the Day of your First Communion
Lift Up Your Hearts

Copyright © 2022 by Sarah Howell. All rights reserved. No part of this book may be reproduced or used in any manner without written permission of the copyright owner. For permission contact: onthedayyouwerebaptized@gmail.com.

How To Use This Book

Traditionally, compline is the final prayer offered at the end of the day. Before compline, light a candle with your family. A candle is a reminder that amidst the darkness, Jesus is the light of the world. A candle also symbolizes the prayers that we offer to God. Even when we have finished praying, the candle continues to burn just as our prayers continue to be heard by God.

As you pray through this book with your child, the goal is to provide your child the opportunity to participate and respond in prayer. The non-bold text is read by the parent, while the bold text is read by the child. If your child is too young to read, then you or another adult can read the bold part. As this becomes a part of your evening routine, your child will begin to learn these prayers and responses by heart and will be able to participate.

An Order for Compline

The Lord Almighty grant us a quiet night and a perfect end.
Amen.

But thou, O Lord, have mercy upon us;
Thanks be to God.

O God, make speed to save us;
O Lord, make haste to help us.
Glory be to the Father, and to the Son, and to the Holy Ghost;
As it was in the beginning, is now, and ever shall be world without end. Amen.

Praise ye the Lord;
The Lord's name be praised.

Psalm 31:1-6

¹In thee, O LORD, have I put my trust;
let me never be put to confusion;
deliver me in thy righteousness.

²Bow down thine ear to me;
make haste to deliver me.

³And be thou my strong rock, and house of defense,
that thou mayest save me.

[4]For thou art my strong rock, and my castle:
be thou also my guide, and lead me for thy Name's sake.

[5]Draw me out of the net that they have laid privily for me;
for thou art my strength.

[6]Into thy hands I commend my spirit;
for thou hast redeemed me, O Lord, thou God of truth.

Glory be to the Father, and to the Son, and to the Holy Ghost;
As it was in the beginning, is now, and ever shall be world without end. Amen.

Matthew 11:28-30

Come unto me, all ye that labour and are heavy laden, and I will give you rest. Take my yoke upon you, and learn of me; for I am meek and lowly in heart: and ye shall find rest unto your souls. For my yoke is easy, and my burden is light.
Thanks be to God.

Into thy hands, O Lord, I commend my spirit;
Into thy hands, O Lord, I commend my spirit;
For thou hast redeemed me, O Lord, thou God of truth.
I commend my spirit.

Glory be to the Father, and to the Son, and to the Holy Ghost
Into thy hands, O Lord, I commend my spirit.

Hymn

Before the ending of the day,
Creator of the world we pray,
That with thy wonted favour thou
Wouldst be our guard and keeper now.

From all ill dreams defend our eyes,
From nightly fears and fantasies
Tread under foot our ghostly foe,
That no pollution we may know.

O Father, that we ask be done,
Through Jesus Christ, thine only Son;
Who, with the Holy Ghost and thee,
Doth live and reign eternally. Amen.

The Nunc Dimittis

Preserve us, O Lord, waking, and guard us sleeping
that we may watch with Christ, and rest in peace.

Lord, now lettest thou thy servant depart in peace
according to thy word.
For mine eyes have seen
thy salvation,
Which thou hast prepared
before the face of all people;
To be a light to lighten the Gentiles
and to be the glory of thy people Israel.
Glory be to the Father, and to the Son,
and to the Holy Ghost;
As it was in the beginning, is now, and ever shall be
world without end. Amen.

Preserve us, O Lord, waking, and guard us sleeping
that we may watch with Christ, and rest in peace.

The Apostles' Creed

I believe in God the Father Almighty,
Maker of heaven and earth:
And in Jesus Christ his only Son our Lord,
Who was conceived by the Holy Ghost,
Born of the Virgin Mary,
Suffered under Pontius Pilate,
Was crucified, dead, and buried,
He descended into hell;
The third day he rose again from the dead,

He ascended into heaven,
And sitteth on the right hand of
God the Father Almighty;
From thence he shall come to judge
the quick and the dead.
I believe in the Holy Ghost;
The holy Catholic Church;
The Communion of Saints;
The Forgiveness of sins;
The Resurrection of the body;
And the Life everlasting. Amen.

The Lord's Prayer

Our Father, who art in heaven,
 hallowed be thy Name, thy kingdom come,
 thy will be done, on earth as it is in heaven.

Give us this day our daily bread.
And forgive us our trespasses, as we forgive
 those who trespass against us.

And lead us not into temptation, but deliver
 us from evil.

For thine is the kingdom, and the power, and
 the glory, for ever and ever. Amen.

Benedictus es, Domine

Blessed art thou, O Lord God of our fathers:
praised and exalted above all for ever.
Blessed art thou for the Name of thy Majesty:
praised and exalted above all for ever.
Blessed art thou in the temple of thy holiness:
praised and exalted above all for ever.

Blessed art thou that beholdest the depths, and dwellest between the Cherubim:
praised and exalted above all for ever.
Blessed art thou on the glorious throne of thy Kingdom:
praised and exalted above all for ever.
Blessed art thou, O Lord, in the firmament of heaven;
praised and exalted above all for ever.

Confession

We confess to God Almighty, the Father, the Son, and the Holy Ghost, that we have sinned in thought, word, and deed, through our own grievous fault. Wherefore we pray God to have mercy upon us.

Almighty God, have mercy upon us, forgive us all our sins and deliver us from all evil, confirm and strengthen us in all goodness, and bring us to life everlasting. Amen.

Lighten our darkness, we beseech thee, O Lord; and by thy great mercy defend us from all perils and dangers of this night; for the love of thy only Son, our Saviour, Jesus Christ. Amen.

We will lay us down in peace and take our rest;
For it is thou, Lord, only that makest us dwell in safety.

The Lord be with you;
And also with you.
Let us bless the Lord.
Thanks be to God.

The Almighty and merciful Lord, the Father, the Son,
and the Holy Ghost; bless and preserve us.
Amen.

Other Books by Sarah Howell on Amazon

On The Day You Were Baptized
On the Day of your First Communion
Lift Up Your Hearts

Copyright © 2022 by Sarah Howell. All rights reserved. No part of this book may be reproduced or used in any manner without written permission of the copyright owner. For permission contact: onthedayyouwerebaptized@gmail.com.

Printed in Great Britain
by Amazon